DAY 1

He who masters himself is the mightiest warrior.

Confucius

DAY 2

The two mightiest warriors are patience and time.

Leo Tolstoy

Natural talent without education has raised more men to virtue and glory than education without natural talent.

Marcus Aurelius

DAY 4

We make war that we may live in peace.

Aristotle

DAY 5

Respect, honesty, courage, rectitude, loyalty, honor, benevolence.

Yamamoto Tsunetomo

DAY 6

Strategy without tactics is the longest way to victory.
Tactics without strategy is the noise before defeat.

Sun-Tzu

DAY 7

Death is nothing, but to live defeated and inglorious
is to die daily.

Napoléon Bonaparte

DAY 8

If a man is as wise as a serpent, he can afford to be as harmless as a dove.

Cheyenne Proverb

DAY 9

Remember, you have no companions but your shadow.

Genghis Khan

DAY 10

A warrior must only make sure his spirit is never broken.

Chozan Shissai

DAY 11

Greatness does not consist in receiving honors but in deserving them.

Aristotle

DAY 12

*In the void there is no evil, only virtue. There is
wisdom and principle. There is the way.*

Miyamoto Musashi

DAY 13

One is not born a warrior, he becomes one.

Arabic Proverb

The man with just a short knife must try, and try again.

Vapnfirðinga Saga

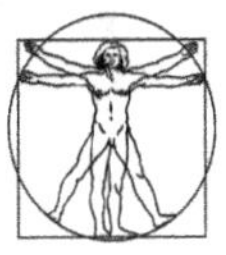

DAY 15

The wise does at once, what the fool does at the end.

Niccolò Machiavelli

Let your plans be as obscure and inscrutable as night, and fall like a thunderbolt, when you act.

Sun-Tzu

In times of war, the law falls silent.

Cicero

Out of hundred men, ten should not even be on the battlefield, eighty are just targets, nine are true fighters and will do the battle. One is a true warrior who will bring the others back.

Heraclitus

The distance between heaven and earth is no greater than one thought.

Mongolian Proverb

If you do not control the enemy, the enemy will control you.

Miyamoto Musashi

There is no good in anything until it is completed.

Genghis Khan

He who lives in harmony with himself lives in harmony with the universe.

Marcus Aurelius

DAY 23

Even the finest sword, plunged into salt water ,will eventually rust.

Sun-Tzu

That which you do not need will kill you.

Tuareg Proverb

Heaven cannot brook two suns, nor earth two masters.

Alexander the Great

DAY 26

You become strong by defying defeat and by turning loss and failure into success.

Napoléon Bonaparte

DAY 27

Where wolf's ears are, wolf's teeth are near.

Volsunga Saga

DAY   28

*Be kind with the person you meet, for everyone is
fighting a hard battle.*

Plato

DAY 29

The most important thing to a warrior's heart is to accomplish one's aim every second of every day.

Yamamoto Tsunetomo

Right action is better than knowledge, yet the right thing cannot be done, without knowing what is right.

Charlemagne

He who shows mercy to the conquered, conquers twice.

Julius Caesar

DAY 32

If you know yourself and not the enemy, you will suffer a defeat for every victory he gains.

Sun-Tzu

DAY 33

The little reed which bends to the force of the wind,
will stand upright, after the storm has passed.

Aesop

Ability will never catch up with the demand for it.

Confucius

DAY 35

Courage leads to the stars, fear to death.

Seneca the Elder

DAY 36

The hammer that shatters glass, forges steel.

Assyrian Proverb

No man is invincible, therefore no one can fully understand what would make a man invincible.

Miyamoto Musashi

Multiplicity in counsel, unity in command.

Cyrus the Great

DAY 39

Once you have made up your mind, stick to it, there is no longer any 'if' or 'but'.

Napoléon Bonaparte

DAY 40

Nothing in the world is more yielding and weak than water, yet nothing is as powerful when it attacks what is hard and strong.

Lao-Tzu

DAY 41

Without training, they lacked knowledge. Without knowledge, they lacked confidence. Without confidence, they lacked victory.

Julius Caesar

DAY 42

Greatness by deeds, not by birth.

Chanakya

DAY 43

A warrior is worthless unless he rises above others and stands strong in the midst of a storm.

Yamamoto Tsunetomo

Better to have less thunder in the mouth and more lightning in the hand.

Apache Proverb

DAY 45

Let us conduct ourselves so that all men wish to be our friends and all are afraid to be our enemies.

Alexander the Great

The supreme art of war is to subdue the enemy without fighting.

Sun-Tzu

Everyone has some friend, even among his enemies.

Olaf Haraldsson's Saga

DAY 48

Nothing can stop you, or hold you back, for your will
is always within your control.

Epictetus

Seek what you value most dearly and bow only to a lofty mountain.

Maori Proverb

I hear and I forget. I see and I remember. I do and I understand.

Confucius

Great ambition is the passion of a great character.
Those endowed with it may perform very good or
very bad acts. All depends on the principles which
direct them.

Napoléon Bonaparte

It is not the oath that makes a man trustworthy, but the man the oath.

Aeschylus

DAY 53

Nothing happens to anybody which he is not fitted
to bear.

Marcus Aurelius

Today you win over yourself, tomorrow over lesser men.

Miyamoto Musashi

DAY 55

Actions come by the use of the legs, and if arrows come, there are legs behind them.

Masai Proverb

There is no easy way from earth to heaven.

Seneca the Younger

*Fear the goat from the front, the horse from the rear
and man from all sides.*

Assyrian Proverb

To become your opponent, put yourself in his place, and think from his point of view.

Miyamoto Musashi

He who wishes to fight must first count the cost.

Sun-Tzu

Cry havoc and let slip the dogs of war!

William Shakespeare

DAY 61

A battle is won by the side that is determined to win.

Leo Tolstoy

Go to the battlefield firmly confident of victory and you will come home with no wounds whatsoever.

Kenshin Uesugi

DAY 63

The facts speak for themselves.

Demosthenes

Fill your bowl to the brim and it will spill. Keep sharpening your knife and it will blunt.

Lao-Tzu

DAY 65

Victory is always easy. We have but to toil awhile, endure awhile, believe always, and never turn back.

Seneca the Elder

One'sactions are often worse than his intentions.

Hrafnkel Freysgothi's Saga

Fall seven times and stand up eight.

Japanese Proverb

It is a common mistake in going to war to begin at the wrong end, act first, and wait for disasters to discuss them.

Thucydides

If you wish to control others you must first control yourself.

Miyamoto Musashi

Nothing is more difficult and therefore more
valuable than be able to take decisions.

Napoléon Bonaparte

The strength of a wall is neither greater nor less than the courage of the men who defend it.

Mongolian Proverb

Once a fight has started, if you get involved in thinking about what to do, you will be cut down by your opponent's very next blow.

Yagyu Munenori

To enjoy the rainbow, deal with the rain.

Emperor Augustus

*The weak warrior wearing sandals, overcomes the
brave with a thorn in his foot.*

Nigerian Proverb

You do not develop courage by being happy in your relationships every day. You develop it by surviving difficult times and challenging adversity.

Epicurus

I dislike death, yet I I dislike some things more than death. Therefore, it is impossible for me to avoid danger all the time.

Mencius

Make no small plans for they have not the power to stir men's blood.

Niccolò Machiavelli

Eagles should show their claws, even in the moment of death.

Olaf Haraldsson's Saga

*You know what you are about to say, but never
what you will be told.*

Masai Proverb

The only reason a warrior is alive is to fight, and the only reason a warrior fights is to win.

Miyamoto Musashi

The most detestable grief is to know the truth and not be able to change the events.

Herodotus

DAY 82

A true warrior, like tea, shows his strength in hot water.

Chinese Proverb

DAY 83

Calmness, not skill, is the sign of a matured warrior.

Tsukahara Bokuden

*Self-control is the chief element in self-respect and
self-respect is the chief element in courage.*

Thucydides

No matter if the enemy has thousands of men, there is fulfillment in simply standing them off and being determined to cut them all down, starting from one end.

Yamamoto Tsunetomo

*If you are afraid, do not do it, if you are doing it - do
not be afraid.*

Genghis Khan

DAY 87

It requires more courage to suffer than to die.

Napoléon Bonaparte

*Great deeds and ill deeds often fall within each
other's shadow.*

Gisli Sursson's Saga

# DAY 89

*Greatness in a leader is measured in part by
your willingness to accept daunting challenges.
Achieving tough goals requires practicing the secret
of commitment: risk all to win all.*

Toyotomi Hideyoshi

Do not show the hawk your bow, or he will fly away.

Masai Proverb

A man who does not plan long ahead will find
trouble at his door.

Confucius

Danger shines like sunshine to a brave man's eyes.

Euripides

Do not beat the drums of war unless you are ready
to fight.

African Proverb.

You may leave behind your body but never your honor.

Miyamoto Musashi

It is more difficult to organize peace than to win a war but the fruits of victory will be lost if the peace is not well organized.

Aristotle

DAY 96

In war, the strong make slaves of the weak, and in peace the rich makes slaves of the poor.

Oscar Wilde

DAY 97

The lover of my enemy is my sword's sheath.

Tibetan Proverb

Find a path or make one.

Seneca the Younger

Every light is not the sun.

Alexander the Great

DAY 100

When the world is at peace, a gentleman keeps his
sword by his side.

Wu-Tsu

Freedom lies in the hands of those brave enough to defend it.

Pericles

The weak are meat, the strong do eat.

Japanese Proverb

The only defense against flattery is making people understand that the truth will not offend you.

Niccolò Machiavelli

The way of a warrior is based on humanity, love, and sincerity, the heart of martial valor is true bravery, wisdom, love, and friendship. Emphasis on the physical aspects of warriorship is futile, for the power of the body is always limited.

Morihei Ueshiba

DAY 105

Take time to deliberate, but when the time of action comes, waste no more time on planning and act.

Napoléon Bonaparle

The bravest men are those who have the clearest vision of what is before them and go to meet it, no matter if danger or glory.

Thucydides

Even if the skies were shorter than my knees, I would not kneel.

Cyrus the Great

DAY 108

Do not fight a lion with a stick.

Masai Proverb

Let your step to be slow and steady, that you stumble not.

Ieyasu Tokugawa

The difficulty is not so great to die for a friend, as to find a friend worth dying for.

Homer

DAY 111

Eat breakfast by yourself, share dinner with your friend, give the supper to your enemy.

Russian Proverb

Think lightly of yourself and deeply of the world.

Miyamoto Musashi

DAY 113

Victorious warriors win first and then go to war, while defeated warriors go to war first and then seek to win.

Sun-Tzu

The road up and the road down are one and the same.

Heraclitus

Brave men rejoice in adversity, just as brave warriors triumph in war.

Seneca the Younger

The way of the warrior is resolute acceptance of death.

Miyamoto Musashi

The shaft of the arrow is feathered with the eagle's plumes. We often provides our enemies the means to destroy us.

Aesop

DAY 118

Those away from the battlefield boast about their swords.

Kurdish Proverb

*When I let go of what I am, I become what I might
be.*

Lao-Tzu

DAY 120

You can never cross the ocean until you have the
courage to lose sight of the shore.

Christopher Columbus

We do not rise to the level of our expectations, we
fall to the level of our training.

Archilochus

You already possess everything necessary to become great.

Crow

The way of the sword is realized in the presence of death. This means choosing death whenever there is a choice between life and death.

Yamamoto Tsunetomo

DAY 124

Our greatest glory is not in never falling, but in rising every time we fall.

Confucius

DAY 125

It is better to be wise, and not to seem so, than to seem wise, and not be so.

Plato

You must not fight too often with one enemy, or you will teach him all your art of war.

Napoléon Bonaparte

In the house of a coward people point at the tomb of yesterday's warrior.

African Proverb

Where wisdom is called for, force is of little use.

Herodotus

He who is brave is free.

Seneca the Younger

Focus on your one purpose.

Japanese Motto

United we stand, divided we fall.

Aesop

If you know the art of breathing you have the strength, wisdom and courage of ten tigers.

Chinese Adage

Without knowledge, skill cannot be focused. Without skill, strength cannot be brought to bear and without strength, knowledge may not be applied.

Alexander the Great's Chief Physician

When lesser men attempt great deeds, they always reduce them to the level of their mediocrity.

Napoléon Bonaparte

Know your enemy, know his sword.

Miyamoto Musashi

It is the way that creates the warrior, each path
leading to peace, every choice to wisdom, and life
will always arise in mystery.

Socrates

A man must make his own arrows.

Winnebago Proverb

Be aware and grateful of the excellences you possess and remember how you would yearn for them if you had them not.

Marcus Aurelius

I need not fear my enemies because the most they can do is attack me. I need not fear my friends because the most they can do is betray me. But I have much to fear from people who are indifferent.

Assyrian Proverb

DAY 140

See first with your mind, then with your eyes, and
finally with your body.

Yagyu Munenori

DAY 141

Victory is reserved for those who are willing to pay its price.

Sun-Tzu

Those whose minds are less sensible to danger and whose hands faster to meet it, are the bravest men.

Thucydides

Let honor be to us as strong an obligation as
necessity is to others.

Pliny the Elder

DAY 144

The first blow is half the battle.

Chinese Proverb

Circumstances rule men, men do not rule circumstances.

Herodotus

Victory belongs to the most persevering one.

Napoléon Bonaparte

Be brave. Suffering, when it climbs the highest, lasts not long.

Aeschylus

DAY 148

The warrior is one who sacrifices himself for the good of others.

Sitting Bull

At heart I am a warrior.

Friedrich Nietzsche

Dog bark at what they do not understand.

Heraclitus

Fire tests gold, adversity tests men.

Seneca the Younger

I choose the likely man in preference to the rich man. I want a man without money rather than money without a man.

Themistocles

DAY 153

Know honor, yet keep humility. Be the valley of
the universe and being the valley of the universe,
ever true and resourceful, return to the state of the
uncarved block.

Lao-Izu

In everyday life make your stance your combat stance.

Miyamoto Musashi

DAY 155

Before all else, be armed.

Niccolò Machiavelli

It takes less courage to criticize the decisions of others than to stand by your own.

Attila the Hun

DAY 157

Over-preparation is the enemy of inspiration.

Napoléon Bonaparte

Arouse a bee and it will come at you with the force of a dragon.

Takeda Shingen

There are many worlds and I have yet to conquer one.

Alexander the Great

DAY 160

Before engaging into battle, plan the retreat.

Chinese Proverb

Fear not death for the hour of your doom is set and none may escape it.

Volunga Saga

A half truth is the worst of all lies, because it can be defended in partiality.

Solon

DAY 164

The secret of all victory lies in the organization of the non-obvious.

Marcus Aurelius

DAY 165

It is difficult to know one's true limits an weaknesses.

Yamamoto Tsunetomo

Everything great thing is not always good, but all good things, are always great.

Demosthenes

He who knows when he can fight and when he
cannot, will be victorious.

Sun-Tzu

All men are alike, yet the best among them are those who have been trained in the most severe school.

Thucydides

When you were born, you cried and the world rejoiced. Live your life so that when you die, the world cries and you rejoice.

Cherokee Proverb

Practice martial arts in a way they will useful anytime and teach them in a way they will be useful in all things.

Miyamoto Musashi

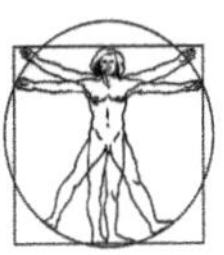

DAY 171

He who owes least to fortune is in the strongest position.

Niccolò Machiavelli

Better to live or die once and for all, than die by inches.

Homer

DAY 173

Small opportunities often presage great enterprises.

Demosthenes

Never trust the smile of your enemy.

Babylonian Saying

Man's enemies are not demons, but human beings like himself.

Lao-Tzu

When the blast of war blows in our ears, then imitate
the action of the tiger.

William Shakespeare

Character is destiny.

Heraclitus

> *It is not death that a man should fear, but he should fear never beginning to live.*
>
> *Marcus Aurelius*

> *There may be a hundred stances and sword positions, but you win with just one.*
>
> Yagyu Munenori

One finger does not kill a louse.

Masai Proverb

Conquering the world on horseback is easy,
dismounting and governing is hard.

Genghis Khan

DAY 183

Never discourage anyone who keeps making progress, no matter how slow.

Aristotle

A drop of sweat spent in training is a drop of blood saved in battle.

Chinese Proverb

*Never walk away from home without your axe and
sword. You can't feel a battle in your bones or
foresee a fight.*

The Havamal

# DAY 186

*Leadership demands confidence and optimism.
Pessimism is always a losing strategy.*

Toyotomi Hideyoshi

DAY 187

Be where your enemy is not.

Sun-Tzu

Success depends on effort.

Sophocles

DAY 189

Strategy is the art of making use of time and space. Space concerns me not, lost time we can never recover.

Napoléon Bonaparte

A tiger wearing a bell will starve.

Mongolian Proverb

DAY 191

A doubtful friend is worse than a certain enemy. Let a man be one thing or the other, and we then know how to meet him.

Aesop

DAY 192

Faced with what is right, to leave it undone is a lack of courage.

Confucius

The important thing about a problem is not its solution, but the strength we gain in finding the solution.

Seneca the Younger

To become the enemy, see yourself as the enemy of the enemy.

Miyamoto Musashi

DAY 195

Water cannot be forced up a hill.

Masai Proverb

Never interrupt an enemy while he is making a mistake.

Napoléon Bonaparte

Not how long but how nobly you live.

Seneca the Younger

Prudence consists in the power to recognize the nature of disadvantages and to take the less disagreeable as good.

Niccolò Machiavelli

Focusing on a single leaf, you will miss the tree.
Focusing on a single tree, you will miss the mountain.

Takuan Soho

Restrain is the manifestation of power that impresses men most.

Thucydides

Ability is useless without opportunity.

Napoléon Bonaparte

DAY 202

Honor always wins, it is unavoidable.

Ishida Mitsunari

DAY 203

Hasten with caution.

Emperor Augustus

If you go and take the field of an enemy, the enemy will come and take your field.

Assyrian Proverb

The person you are matters more than the place you go.

Seneca the Younger

Great deeds are usually wrought at great risks.

Herodotus

The greatest enemy will hide in the last place you would ever look.

Julius Caesar

Life is conquering the fear of death within one's mind. Empty the mind, make a hazard, and overcome the enemy with a single powerful slash.

Takenaka Shigekata

What you leave behind in woven in the life of others, not engraved in stone monuments.

Pericles

When facing an enemy, is better to have a stout heart than a sharp sword.

Volsunga Saga

Overcoming evil, not defeating an opponent, is the true essence of swordmanship.

Yagyu Munenori

Most things are brought to success by a calm and cautious forethought, rather than by impetuous ambition.

Thucydides

The goal of the way of the sword is to be fearless when facing both our inner and outer enemies.

Tesshu Yamaoka

Will be victorious he who prudently lies in wait for an enemy that does not.

Sun-Tzu

You can learn from anyone, even your enemy.

Ovid

It is the nature of mortals to kick a fallen man.

Aeschylus

*Do not underestimate the power of an enemy,
no matter how great or small, to rise against you
another day.*

Attila the Hun

Foxes are hunted by hiding, wolves by facing them openly.

Seneca The Younger

DAY 219

Leaders can be wrong but they cannot be unclear.

Toyotomi Hideyoshi

One should always go before his enemies with confidence, otherwise his apparent uneasiness inspires them with greater boldness.

Napoléon Bonaparte

Do not draw your sword to kill a fly.

Korean Proverb

Do every act of your life as if it were your last.

Marcus Aurelius

DAY 223

> *The one who learns and learns and does not practice is like the one who plows and plows and never plants.*
>
> Plato

DAY 224

A thousand warriors are easy to find. The hard thing
is to find one good general.

Chinese Proverb

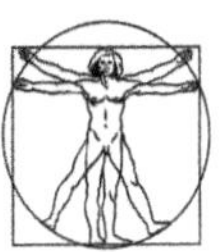

DAY 225

A man who tries to be good all the times, will be crushed by the number of those who are not.

Niccolò Machiavelli

To realize the true way of the sword, know the smallest and the biggest things, the shallowest, and the deepest.

Miyamoto Musashi

DAY 227

Suffering inflicted by chaos should be borne
with perseverance, that inflicted by enemy with
courage.

Thucydides

Beware of the man who does not talk, and the dog that does not bark.

Cheyenne Proverb

The art of living well and of dying well are one and
the same.

Epicurus

Teachers open the doors, pupils enter by themselves.

Chinese Proverb

DAY 231

Want of sense, courage, and vigilance, are among the greatest failings.

Thucydides

Men who respond to good fortune with modesty and kindness are harder to find than those who face adversity with courage.

Cyrus the Great

DAY 233

Fight determined to die and you will survive. Fight wishing to survive and you will surely meet death.

Uesugi Kenshin

No friend ever served me, and no enemy ever wronged me, whom I have not repaid in full.

Sulla

DAY 235

It does not matter how slowly you go so long as you do not stop.

Confucius

Those who voluntarily put power into the hands of a tyrant or an enemy, must not wonder if it be at last turned against themselves.

Aesop

Matters of great concern should be treated lightly.
Matters of small concern should be treated seriously.

Yamamoto Tsunetomo

If you want a thing done well, do it yourself.

Napoléon Bonaparte

We are more often frightened than hurt, and we suffer more from imagination than from reality.

Seneca the Elder

Life is not so important when forced to choose between life and integrity.

Yamamoto Tsunetomo

To take up great resolutions, and then to lay them aside, only ends in dishonor.

King Olaf Trygvisson's Saga

Creating without claiming, doing without taking credit, guiding without interfering, This is primal virtue.

Lao-Tzu

Better have a stout heart and bear one's share of suffering, than ever fearing what may happen.

Herodotus

A problem is solved by continuing to find solutions.

Maori Proverb

What is done well is done fast enough.

Emperor Augustus

DAY 246

When a way reaches its end, change, and the
change will lead you through.

I-Ching

The focused mind can pierce through stone.

Japanese Proverb

All men's gains are the fruit of venturing.

Herodotus

The undisturbed mind is like the calm body water reflecting the brilliance of the moon. Empty the mind and you will realize the undisturbed mind.

Yagyu Jubei Mitsuyoshi

Draw not your bow till your arrow is fixed.

Russian Proverb

DAY 251

Injuries may be forgiven, but are never forgotten.

Aesop

There is something noble in hearing myself ill spoken of, when I am doing well.

Alexander the Great

DAY 253

*Appear weak when you are strong, and strong
when you are weak.*

Sun-Tzu

Adversity draws out the qualities of a man that otherwise would have laid dormant.

Herodotus

DAY 255

In strategy, see distant things as they were close and those which are close as they were afar.

Miyamoto Musashi

A desperate disease requires a dangerous remedy.

Guy Fawkes

A leader is a dealer in hope.

Napoléon Bonaparte

The best sword is the one left in the scabbard.

Japanese Proverb

DAY 259

There are two types of men: those who move forward and achieve things and those who follow and criticize.

Seneca the Younger

DAY 260

It often happens that he who gets a death wound
yet avenges himself.

The Story of Hreidar the Fool

DAY 261

[When] two tigers fight, one will surely get hurt.

Chinese Proverb

Remember upon the conduct of each depends the
fate of all.

Alexander the Great

Impossible is a word found only in the dictionary of fools.

Napoléon Bonaparte

You must understand that there is more than one
path to the top of a mountain.

Miyamoto Musashi

Those who can think, but cannot express what they think, place themselves at the level of those who cannot think.

Pericles

DAY 266

The greatest danger is not having aims so high we cannot reach, but so low we will accomplish.

Michelangelo

A great warrior fights on his own terms or not at all.

Sun-Tzu

Discriminated men will be seen as schemers, far-sighted ones as cowards, and those with a rough behavior as true warriors.

Takeda Shingen

Wise men talk about ideas, intellectuals about facts, and the commoners about what he eats.

Mongolian Proverb

He who wants peace must prepare for war.

Claudius

Spirit is the sword, experience the sharpening stone.

Arab Proverb

You can only fight the way you practice.

Miyamoto Musashi

DAY 273

If you have to loaves of bread eat one to nourish the body and sell the other to buy hyacinths to nourish the spirit.

Herodotus

> *You will never know how far you can fly until you spread your wings.*
>
> *Napoléon Bonaparte*

You can prevent your opponent from defeating you through defense, but you cannot defeat him without taking the offensive.

Sun-Tzu

One should make his decisions within the space of seven breaths.

Yamamoto Tsunetomo

Hard things to bear are sweet to remember.

Seneca the Younger

Fight your foes in the field, nor be burnt in your house.

Volsunga Saga

Be both a speaker of words and a doer of deeds.

Homer

It is easy to hide from a revealed sword, but hard to guard against a hidden arrow.

Chinese Proverb

To know ten thousand things, know one well.

Miyamoto Musashi

Anybody can become angry - that is easy, but
to be angry with the right person and to the right
degree and at the right time and for the right
purpose, and in the right way - that is not within
everybody's power and is not easy.

Aristotle

DAY 283

An angry man is again angry with himself when he returns to reason.

Publilius Syrus

Not to borrow the strength of another, nor to rely
on one's own strength, to cut off past and future
thoughts, and not to live within the everyday mind...
then the great way is right before your eyes.

Yamamoto Tsunetomo

Untroubled, scornful, outrageous - that is how wisdom wants us to be: she is a woman and never loves anyone but a warrior.

Friedrich Nietzsche

It is part of human nature to hate the man you have hurt.

Tacitus

The ultimate aim of martial arts is not having to use them.

Miyamoto Musashi

If you have no knowledge of yourself and of your
enemy you surely are in peril.

Sun-Tzu

Ten warriors wisely led will beat a hundred without a head.

Euripides

It is because of man we wear swords.

Tshi Proverb

DAY 291

*We do not dare not because things are difficult,
things are difficult because we do not dare.*

Seneca the Younger

As a warrior, I must strengthen my character, as a human being I must perfect my spirit.

Yamaoka Tesshu

How many things apparently impossible have nevertheless been performed by resolute men who had no alternative but death.

Napoléon Bonaparte

Hope is an expensive luxury. It makes better sense to be prepared.

Thucydides

An active soul is a healthy soul.

Maori Proverb

When we see persons of worth, we should think of equaling them, when we see persons of a contrary character, we should turn inwards and examine ourselves.

Confucius

The coward calls the brave man rash, the rash calls him a coward.

Aristotle

Never stray from the way.

Miyamoto Musashi

The best revenge is to be unlike him who performed
the injury.

Marcus Aurelius

DAY 300

The strong man is the one who is able to intercept at will the communication between the senses and the mind.

Napoléon Bonaparte

The way lies at hand yet it is sought afar off, the thing lies in the easy yet it is sought in the difficult.

Mencius

Good warriors take position on a ground where they cannot lose, and never overlook the condition that lead to the enemy's defeat.

Sun-Tzu

Good fortune is the greatest of blessings, but good counsel comes next, and the lack of it destroys the other also.

Demosthenes

Better to fight and fall than to live without hope.

Volsunga Saga

Let the sword decide once the strategy has failed.

Arabic Proverb

*When you surround an army, leave an outlet free.
Do not press a desperate foe too hard.*

Sun-Tzu

Better do nothing than do ill.

Pliny the Elder

In all things that you do, consider the end.

Solon

Get beyond love and grief: exist for the good of man.

Miyamoto Musashi

The art of living is more like wrestling than dancing.

Marcus Aurelius

There are in the world two powers the sword and the spirit. The spirit has always vanquished the sword.

Napoléon Bonaparte

DAY 312

Be the chief but never the lord.

Lao-Tzu

DAY 313

Moral excellence comes about as a result of habit.
We become just by doing just acts, temperate by
doing temperate acts, brave by doing brave acts.

Aristotle

The cherry blossom among flowers, the warrior among men.

Japanese Proverb

I possess a high art, I hurt with cruelty those who would damage me.

Archilochus

For my words are my own, and my actions are my ministers.

Charles II

If you allow others use you for your purposes, they will use you for theirs.

Aesop

To give a person an opinion one must first judge well whether that person is of the disposition to receive it or not.

Yamamoto Tsunetomo

Before embarking on a journey of revenge, dig two graves.

Confucius

Throw off your worries when you throw off your clothes at night.

Napoléon Bonaparte

DAY 321

Reject your sense of injury and the injury itself
disappears.

Marcus Aurelius

Wise to resolve, and patient to perform.

Homer

DAY 323

Even if you are certain to lose, retaliate.

Yamamoto Tsunetomo

A hungry wolf is bound to wage a hard battle.

Laxdaela Saga

Every new beginning comes from some other
beginning's end.

Seneca the Elder

It is a bad plan that admits of no modification.

Publilius Syrus

When a match has equal partners then I fear not.

Aeschylus

The teacher is as a needle, the disciple as a thread.

Miyamoto Musashi

I am not afraid of an army of lions led by a sheep, I am afraid of an army of sheep led by a lion.

Alexander the Great

Laugh at your problems, everybody else does.

Seneca the Younger

Honor may not win power, but it wins respect. And respect earns power.

Ishida Mitsunari

The most dangerous moment comes with victory.

Napoléon Bonaparte

Having knowledge but lacking the power to express it clearly is no better than never having any ideas at all.

Pericles

*When it is obvious that the goals cannot be
reached, do not adjust the goals, adjust the action
steps.*

Confucius

DAY 335

Sheer effort enables those with nothing to surpass those with privilege and position.

Toyotomi Hideyoshi

When you arise in the morning, think of what a precious privilege it is to be alive, to breathe, to think, to enjoy, to love.

Marcus Aurelius

*One should warn even a dim-witted troll if he sits
naked by a fire.*

Heitharvega Saga

Fast as the wind, quiet as a forest, aggressive as fire, and immovable as a mountain.

Japanese Proverb

DAY 339

Violence, even well intentioned, always rebounds upon oneself.

Lao-Tzu

It is from the greatest dangers that the greatest glory is to be won.

Thucydides

All men are equal but for the their belief in themselves, regardless of what others think.

Miyamoto Musashi

[When] one man is ready to risk his life ten thousand men cannot defeat him.

Chinese Proverb

DAY 343

A dead man cannot bite.

Pompey

Forethought we may have, undoubtedly, but not foresight.

Napoléon Bonaparte

No beast is more savage than man when he
possesses the power to equal his rage.

Plutarch

A warrior will use a toothpick even though he has not eaten. Inside the skin of a dog, outside the hide of a tiger.

Yamamoto Tsunetomo

The man who never test himself against adversity is the most unhappy, for he is not permitted to prove himself.

Seneca the Younger

In dire moments even the very powerful have need of the weakest.

Aesop

It is difficult to take a wolf cub without bringing in the whole pack.

Mongolian Proverb

Great results, can be achieved with small forces.

Sun-Tzu

Better die standing than live kneeling.

Pericles

Step by step walk the thousand-mile road.

Miyamoto Musashi

DAY 353

Truth is always the first casualty of war.

Aeschylus

Never give a sword to a man who can't dance.

Confucius

DAY 355

The warrior's intention should be simply to grasp his sword and to die.

Kiyomasa Kato

*The first virtue in a warrior is endurance of fatigue.
Courage is only the second virtue.*

Napoléon Bonaparte

I have no sword, I make absence of self my sword.

Japanese Proverb

> *If one is skilled but unwilling to perform, he is malevolent.*
>
> *Epicurus*

Knowledge is nothing more than potential. Applying knowledge is power, understanding how and why do it is wisdom.

Takeda Shingen

Courage is not having the strength to go on. It is going on when you do not have strength.

Napoléon Bonaparte

DAY 361

Our passions, just like water and fire, are good servants, but bad masters.

Aesop

Those who know how to win are much more numerous than those who know how to make proper use of their victories.

Polybius

Wake early if you want another man's life or land.
No lamb for the lazy wolf. No battle's won in bed.

The Havamal

DAY 365

Nothing can be achieved without a plan, workforce
and way of doing things.

Maori Proverb

Created and designed by Zenith Books

Warrior Daytimer Pocket - 365 Quotes from Ancient Wisdom © 2018-19 Blue Monkey Studio

(under proprietary publishing line Zenith Books)

Quotes' translation & adaptation by C. Sesselego

Icons & Cover design by L. Livi

Cover image @ 2017-19 Blue Monkey Studio (used with permission)

Zenith Books

www.zenithbooks.eu